C000099852

53
women

53

women

~~you don't know~~
who changed
our world

(well, you might do)

anon.

ONWE
PRESS

First published in Great Britain in 2020 by Onwe Press Ltd
This hardback edition was first published in 2020

Printed and bounded by Clays Printers (UK) Ltd.

Illustrations by Natalia Burlaka
Cover Design by Mariam Jimoh

A CIP catalogue record for this book is
available from the British Library.

Hardback ISBN 978-1-9160429-4-0

*I would venture to guess that anon,
who wrote so many poems without signing them,
was often a woman – Virginia Woolf*

CONTENTS

FOODIES & CONNOISSEURS 45

LEADING LADIES 57

MEDIA MOGULS 67

POWERHOUSES 91

CONTENTS

INTRODUCTION

History is important. "You can't know where you're going until you know where you've come from." The greats have been saying that for years. From Maya Angelou to Martin Luther King to Shakespeare himself, all have sung its praises. But as important as history is, it is incomplete.

And it will always be incomplete.

Award-winning historian Dr Bettany Hughes points out that in our 5,000-years of recorded history, women occupy a measly 0.5%. Doesn't this seem a bit low for over half of the world's population? That's because it is. Shockingly low.

Centuries of patriarchal rule have resulted in a deliberate fingers-in-ear-eyes-shut approach to women's contributions to the buildings we live in, the cars we drive, the food we eat, the movies we watch and music we enjoy . . . and to much more than we can ever imagine. As the world continues to ignore women, more and more girls grow up doubtful of their capabilities. This debilitating trait has contributed to every woman's life, including things like the equal pay gap, lagging women's rights and the #MeToo movement.

We think enough is enough. It is time to rewrite history and, in so doing, ensure that women's futures are brighter than their past.

We are introducing you to 53 women. 53 women who have changed the world. 53 women whose stories will not be lost. And with this, we hope to inspire the next generation of world-changing women who we hope will not be unheard, underestimated or forgotten.

We hope you enjoy their fascinating stories and give voice to their remarkable contributions. After all, history is important.

THE ARTS

PAULA MODERSOHN-BECKER
1876-1907

The Twentieth Century Impressionist Painter
Who Gave Us The First Nude

NATIONALITY	STAR SIGN	MOON SIGN
German	*Aquarius*	*Pisces*

> *"It seems to me that you have shed too much of your old self*
> *and spread it out like a cloak so that your king can walk on*
> *it. I wish for your sake, and for the world, and for art . . . that*
> *you would wear your own golden cape again."*

Paula Modersohn-Becker was one of the early pioneers for expressionism, a modernist movement that changed the way that we viewed art. The well-travelled artist was daring and passionate, spending her time between Germany and Paris and producing an unprecedented eighty paintings a year. The majority of Modersohn-Becker's paintings were centred on women, often in the nude, a ground-breaking decision in the early 1900s. She soon went on to create the first nude self-portrait by a woman in Europe, depicting the female body in a refreshing and unembellished fashion, a first in her age. Despite her impact, Paula Modersohn-Becker was not widely known at the time of her death and would have likely been lost to obscurity if she hadn't been such a proficient writer. She wrote volumes of diary posts and correspondence that detailed her life and contributions, including her struggle with choosing between motherhood and her career, an all too familiar debate a century on, as well as a torrid affair with a French man!

YAYOI KUSAMA

1929-

*The Woman in the Red Wig, Still Storming
the Art-World at the Age of 90*

NATIONALITY	STAR SIGN	MOON SIGN
Japanese	*Aries*	*Leo*

*"It feels good to be an outsider . . .
I am so absorbed in living my life."*

From a young age, the eccentric Yayoi was plagued with mental illness, particularly in the form of hallucinations. However, this gave her inspiration for her paintings and an avenue to process her visions. After spending the past four decades in a psychiatric hospital, with her name written out of art history, Yayoi Kusama became an art-world phenomenon in the age of the selfie. At 89, she has become world-renowned relatively late in her career but has taken the world (and Instagram) by storm. With large-scale solo shows of her work in Mexico City, Rio, Seoul, Taiwan and Chile, as well as major touring exhibitions in the US and Europe, as well as opening her own five-storey gallery in Tokyo, she reminds us that when you focus on expressing your art alone, it will eventually pay off. Being a self-proclaimed outsider who can't be put in any box is exactly the sort of inspiration we all need.

ZANELE MUHOLI

1972-

The Activist Rewriting Visual Art As We Know It

NATIONALITY	STAR SIGN	MOON SIGN
South African	*Cancer*	*Scorpio*

> *"I always think to myself, if you don't see your community,*
> *you have to create it. I can't be dependent on other*
> *people to do it for us."*

Zanele Muholi is on an incredible mission. They are using their art to document what they describe as a black, queer and trans visual history of South Africa, thereby highlighting the issues this community continually faces in the world. Zanele's work has been described as poignant, bold and confrontational and has inspired a walk-out or two in its day. But despite threats and pushbacks, Zanele refuses to back down. This unstoppable artist is determined to reimagine black identity in ways that are largely personal but inevitably political. They challenge the stereotypes and oppressive standards of beauty that often ignore people of colour. Their work focuses on race, gender and sexuality, with a body of work featuring black, lesbian, gay, transgender, and intersex participants. Zanele didn't stopped there, they co-founded the Forum for the Empowerment of Women, which advocates for the rights of black lesbians in South Africa, as well as Inkanyiso, a collective for queer activism and visual media. Zanele's sense of community runs deep, and they can often be found funding LGBT weddings, funerals, sports teams and courses. That's what we call a truly majestic spirit!

YUU WATASE

1970-

The Manga Artist Who Revamped An Industry

NATIONALITY	STAR SIGN	MOON SIGN
Japanese	*Pisces*	*Aquarius*

"People are like flowers — they don't all have to be the same. Everything blooms according to its own nature."

Yuu Watase's stories have gripped an entire industry for years now. Through a range of comics and manga, they have spun compelling, realistic and romantic manga. They have gained international fame for their mystical, romantic manga TV series called "Mystery Game", which is now considered to be one of the best TV series in the history of anime. Yuu Watase's influence is notable, with their unique manga-style illustrations subtly changing the industry style!

THE BOSSES

ARLAN HAMILTON

1980-

*The Investor Funding Women, LGBTQ,
and Minority Entrepreneur-led projects*

NATIONALITY	STAR SIGN	MOON SIGN
American	*Scorpio*	*Cancer*

> *"I didn't come here to get your pity or your charity.
> I came here to go toe-to-toe with you, head-to-head
> with you, and to take it all."*

Arlan Hamilton built Backstage Capital from the ground up in 2015, an impressive feat for a self-taught entrepreneur without a college degree or wealthy network—and even more impressive once you factor in that Hamilton was homeless at the time! Hamilton discovered that less than 10% of venture capital deals went to women, people of colour and LGBTQ founders, so she worked to change those statistics by creating her own venture capital fund. So far, Backstage Capital has invested over $7M in more than 120 companies led by underrepresented founders. A modern-day Robin Hood without having to steal a dime!

AUDREY GELMAN

LAUREN KASSAN

1987-

1987-

*The Women Who Have Carved Out Safe,
Supportive Spaces For Other Women*

NATIONALITY	STAR SIGN	MOON SIGN
American	*Gemini*	*Leo*
American	*Virgo*	*Scorpio*

*"I don't really care if men moan that these small clubs
are 'sexist'. The whole world is a men's club."*

The Wing started as the brainchild of Audrey Gelman who, fed up with the turmoil of having to change outfits in dingy public toilets, sought out a space for women recalibrate between business meetings. Gelman and Kassan soon fleshed out the concept of The Wing, a safe space dedicated to advancing the civic, professional, economic and social scope for women. As of now, $118m has been poured into the exclusive club, with investments from the likes of Serena Williams, Valerie Jarrett, and members of the US women's soccer team. There's no question that the self-proclaimed "accelerator" for the feminist revolution has made quite a mark on the world.

DEBBIE WOSSKOW OBE

1974-

ANNA JONES

1975-

*The Women Ensuring That Every Woman
Has A Room Of Their Own*

NATIONALITY	STAR SIGN	MOON SIGN
British	*Aquarius . . . we think*	*Definitely a Taurus*
British	*Must be a Pisces*	*We're guessing . . . Capricorn!*

*"When women have 50/50 representation,
then we'll hang up our stilettos."*

Debbie Wosskow and Anna Jones have built a powerhouse of fearless women entrepreneurs through their women-only private members' club, AllBright. They were inspired by their own experiences, both noting the shockingly low number of women in top business positions—a problem they were determined to solve with sisterhood. Debbie and Anne are both motivated to create and give women access to a new ecosystem of capital, connections and confidence, something that men have in abundance. Not ones to hide their ambition, these ladies are determined to take it all and then some!

ELIZABETH HOBBS KECKLEY
1818-1907

The Woman Who Sewed Her
Way To The White House

NATIONALITY	STAR SIGN	MOON SIGN
American	*Aquarius*	*Leo*

"Here, as in all things pertaining to life,
I can afford to be charitable."

Elizabeth Hobbs was a slave-turned-entrepreneur. From a young age, she was taught the important skill of sewing by her mother. As she grew older, she became a very accomplished seamstress and often had to support her slave owners with her income. Eventually, Elizabeth was able to buy her freedom and set up her own business for prominent politicians' wives, which included Abraham Lincoln's wife, who she became very close friends with. Elizabeth's success as a seamstress is not the only notable thing about this incredible businesswoman.

Elizabeth also set up a Contraband Relief Association, which aided newly freed slaves as they made their way to the capital. It's safe to say that with her masterful stitches, Elizabeth was able to help transform the tapestry of the United States!

ELIZABETH MAGIE

1866-1948

*The Woman Who Wrote Her
Own Rules To The Game*

NATIONALITY	STAR SIGN	MOON SIGN
American	*Taurus*	*Cancer*

*"I am thankful that I was taught how to think
and not what to think."*

Elizabeth Magie was a woman far ahead of her time. She defied societal expectations by delaying marriage until her early forties, choosing instead to support herself by writing poetry, short stories and comedic routines. She channelled her distaste for current affairs and created a board game called "The Landlord", known today as "Monopoly". The game was initially created as a critical take on the big monopolists of the era. The game was made with two sets of rules, an anti-monopolist set and a monopolist set. This approach was useful in demonstrating the immoral actions of monopolists. While Elizabeth invented "The Landlord" decades before Charles Darrow, the man ultimately credited and compensated for the game, she is often deliberately written out of history. She ultimately made a meagre $500 out of the game that still remains a staple in homes over a century after its conception!

EMILY WEISS

1985-

From Super Intern to Super (Business) Woman

NATIONALITY	STAR SIGN	MOON SIGN
American	*Aries*	*Aries*

*"I've spent my life relying on lightbulb
moments and jumping in full force."*

Initially introduced to the world during a season on The Hills, a TV show that saw her nicknamed as the Super Intern, Emily has become an inspiration to everyone. Just over a decade later, she continues to display the same charisma and no-excuses, hard-working spirit that earned her that title in founding and running Glossier, a unique beauty brand slash tech company. Revolutionising the beauty shopping experience by "co-creating with their consumers", Emily began with a well-loved blog and grew it into a billion-dollar company. Glossier brought in a million new customers last year and earned over $100 million in revenue. She is a lover of British sweets and candy.

HUDA KATTAN
1983-

The Beauty Influencer Building an Empire

NATIONALITY	STAR SIGN	MOON SIGN
Iraqi-American	*Libra*	*Leo*

"Remember, words are powerful and can have a profound effect, which is why it's so important to be your own cheerleader and let your words lift you up!"

Huda Kattan is a Middle-Eastern mogul redefining the beauty industry. This amazing woman began her billion-dollar makeup empire in 2010 with a blog where she posted tips, DIY makeup tricks and unbiased reviews. This morphed into an incredible makeup brand that is currently gearing up to take on the heavyweights, such as Estée Lauder. Huda Kattan's impressive empire has arguably placed Dubai on the map in terms of beauty, and her stunning headquarters alone stands out as a women-first beacon of light overlooking the Burj Khalifa. Huda is a prime example of the greatness that results from following your dreams. She gave up a career in finance to follow her true passion for makeup—a move that no doubt added more glam to the world!

CONTENT CREATORS

JACKIE AINA

1987-

The Makeup Mastermind Advocating For Us All

NATIONALITY	STAR SIGN	MOON SIGN
American	*Leo*	*Scorpio*

> *"It's been about making myself visible in a time where I wasn't and felt like we weren't."*

Jackie Aina has captured the hearts and minds of many through her work as a beauty guru advocating for inclusivity in the beauty industry. Jackie, or "JackieJackieJackie" for those who can't escape her hilariously catchy theme song, is bringing together beauty and inclusivity—an incredible feat in a world that often denies those who do not fit into the mainstream mould—by acknowledging their own true beauty. She has championed the need to "fill the gaps" in beauty brands who notably "launch twenty shades of beige" but completely miss out on darker shades and diverse undertones. Jackie has been vocal about using her platform to make black women visible in a space that often overlooks women of colour. Throughout the years, Jackie has not only shown us that beauty is more than just skin deep, but also helped us to look our best with amazing and innovative makeup tips!

PATRICIA BRIGHT

1987-

*The Creative Inspiring Millions
With A Chat And A Cuppa Tea*

NATIONALITY	STAR SIGN	MOON SIGN
British	*Aquarius*	*Taurus*

> *"Think of every experience—good or bad—
> as a stepping-stone to the next opportunity."*

From banker to influencer, Patricia Bright started out with nothing, but the self-professed hustler says she used this to fuel her drive to succeed. Patricia's childhood was not always a smooth road. From her father's deportation to having to deal with racism, the beauty blogger had to learn tough lessons early on in life. Luckily, her mother's strength became a source of inspiration. Patricia Bright hustled her way into the corporate world before transforming her vlogging hobby a full-fledged business that today boasts nearly three million subscribers on YouTube, an inspirational book and an amazing podcast. Patricia Bright has shared her unique and warm light with the world whilst taking us along with her on her inspiring journey. With her vulnerability and openness, Patricia has shown millions of people how they too can achieve a life that is authentically theirs. Known for her chatty videos that at times require a tea break, Patricia Bright has become a beautiful friend to millions across the globe.

FOODIES & CONNOISSEURS

EMMA RICE

1974-

The Woman Adding A Dash Of Sparkle
To The British Wine Industry

NATIONALITY	STAR SIGN	MOON SIGN
British	*Aries*	*Cancer*

"I know what I want and, so far,
have managed to achieve it."

Emma Rice is the remarkable woman navigating the male-dominated wine industry. She has taken the sector by storm as the director of Hattingley Valley, one of the largest sparkling wine makers in England. She started her career in imports and oenology before setting up her own wine analysis lab and eventually settling down at Hattingley. Her award-winning wine has earned her the impressive title of one of the most influential women in the wine-making business. What advice does she give to wine-drinkers around the world? "Be as adventurous as your budget allows." Coming from the woman who literally wrote the book on wine, you don't have to tell us twice!

GARIMA ARORA

1986-

The First Indian Female Michelin Starred Chef in the World Who Never Cooks At Home

---

NATIONALITY	STAR SIGN	MOON SIGN
Indian	*Scorpio*	*Pisces*

"Working, to me, is the only truth."

With a passion for her home country, Garima is one of the leading chefs attempting to change the perception of Indian food and techniques. And more than this, she's putting the work in to make it happen with her non-profit initiative, Food Forward India. Garima owns "Gaa", a Michelin-star restaurant in Bangkok, which she describes as not Indian and not Thai but something completely new and different that nobody has tasted before. Behind each dish are old, historical Indian techniques, and the unique use and development of these techniques is likely to be the edge that earned Garima the award of elit™ Vodka Asia's Best Female Chef 2019. She sees Indian cuisine eventually having the same usage and documentation globally as French cuisine. Her no-nonsense approach means she believes hard work is the key to everything, and if she could go back in life, she would only start working harder earlier. One thing we may all have in common with this phenomenal artist is that she never cooks at home and has a secret weakness for nachos. We feel you, Garima.

NTSIKI BIYELA

1978-

The Winemaker Changing A Corked Industry

NATIONALITY	STAR SIGN	MOON SIGN
South African	*Pisces*	*Aquarius*

"I've learned to relate to anyone from anywhere across the board, and with that came the understanding that drives me to be where I want to be."

Ntsiki Biyela is an undeniably remarkable woman. We say this because it takes a special type of woman to fall into one of the most elitist industries as a novice . . . and then take it by storm! Originally from the rural areas of Kwazulu-Natal, Ntsiki jumped at the chance of a scholarship to attend a winery school, despite never having had a sip of wine or speaking a word of the language that the course would be taught in! In her own words: "I had no idea what they were talking about. I heard the word study, and then I was like, 'I'll do it'". As fate would allow, Ntsiki's natural inclination to the trade saw her ascending to the top of her nation's wine industry, winning South Africa's honoured Michelangelo award for her inaugural red blend, as well as South Africa's 2019 Woman Winemaker award. In due time, Ntsiki started her own company, Asilina, named after her dear grandmother. After years in the business, one question still plays on Ntsiki's mind, "where are the women?!" The wine expert remains focused on increasing diversity in the wine space, something she feels will propel the industry further—and we can say cheers to that!

PIM TECHAMUANVIVIT

1971-

*The Chef Bringing Fiery Authenticity
Back To Thai Food*

NATIONALITY	STAR SIGN	MOON SIGN
Thai	*Pisces*	*Gemini*

*"I realised that if I was going to live my life in the U.S.,
I needed to learn how to cook all the dishes that I missed
because no one else was going to do it for me."*

Pim Techamuanvivit started her journey as a foodie. The award-winning chef left her job as a Silicon Valley executive to start a food blog that soon spiralled into a Thai-infused sensation, leading to a book deal and her very own restaurant. Pim soon went from eating at Michelin-star restaurants to earning one herself with Kin Khao, the San Francisco-based restaurant described as authentically Thai and fiery. The Bangkok native learnt of the news whilst battling breast cancer, picking up her award in a wheelchair as she "wasn't going to miss it for the world." Pim has since gone on to become the head chef at one of Asia's best restaurants, Nahm. Pim continues to credit her success and understanding of food to others, claiming "a lot of people call me self-taught, but I learned from everybody. Everyone was my teacher". What started her on this whirlwind journey? Hunger! She claims that her unadulterated love for food has kept her winning at this game, and with a motto like "keep eating, learning, and keep cooking" we can certainly see why!

RUTH ROGERS

1949-

*The Woman Who Pushed The Limits
Of The British Culinary Scene*

NATIONALITY	STAR SIGN	MOON SIGN
British	*Cancer*	*Leo*

*"Times are definitely changing in that respect,
but it's up to us to continue to insist change happens."*

Ruth Rogers is the self-taught chef who gave us the River Café, a staple in Hammersmith, London for over thirty years. The top-tier chef co-founded the iconic Italian restaurant alongside Rose Gray, who sadly passed away in 2010. The globetrotting women started the restaurant after trips abroad left them burning to bring the flavoursome cuisine they found in Italy back to the streets of London. You wouldn't know by its present success, but the restaurant didn't have the smoothest of starts. Not only were the pair limited to day openings, but they were also restricted to only serving those who worked in the community. It's no wonder that the famed River Café didn't make money in its first five years in business! Ruth has weathered many storms throughout the years, from sexism to a catastrophic fire to tragically losing her business partner and her son in back-to-back years. In spite of this, the ironclad woman still steers this magnificent ship with true grace. Not only has she ensured the restaurant's continued success, but she also champions sustainability in supermarket wastage, supports domestic violence refugees and raises money for disasters within the community. Through her leadership, the restaurant boasts a Michelin star and over 70,000 cookbooks sold. From the handwritten menus to the signature pink stove and locally sourced food, it's no doubt that Ruth has made the River Cafe the place to be!

55

LEADING
LADIES

ELLEN JOHNSON SIRLEAF
1938

*The Woman Who Put Liberia
Back On Its Feet*

NATIONALITY	STAR SIGN	MOON SIGN
Liberian	*Scorpio*	*Capricorn*

"If your dreams do not scare you, they are not big enough."

Ellen worked her way up to become the second female president of Liberia, all whilst raising her four children. Before the presidency, Ellen made a name for herself as the Assistant Minister of Finance and was known for her personal financial integrity. Her bold, critical nature often led to clashes with heads of state and also got her imprisoned twice! She was able to bypass execution, but she ultimately paid the price for being a woman with a "fiery" personality with a whopping twelve-year exile sentence. After a couple of failed attempts, she eventually found herself in the presidential seat, where she worked tirelessly to keep peace in a fragile Liberia, as well as advocating for increased women's rights and protection. Dubbed Africa's Iron Lady, we can't help but love a woman who doesn't give up!

WOMAN CHIEF

1806-1854

The Two-Spirit Warrior Queen
Who Took No Prisoners

NATIONALITY
Native American

STAR SIGN
If we have to guess,
we say Scorpio

MOON SIGN
Aries ... definitely
Aries

"I vow to kill one hundred enemies
before I wed any man." *

Woman Chief was one of the most significant leaders for the Native American Crow Tribe in the 19th century. Taken as a prisoner by the Crow Tribe when she was just ten years old, this young warrior soon soared up the ranks, negotiating peace deals and organising successful raids in her twenty-year stint as the tribe's chief. Woman Chief, who ended up wedding four wives, was thought to be a "Two-Spirit", a gender-variant individual—although, atypically, she only wore women's clothing. Her life was full of intense violence, sex and action, and we can't wait until someone wises up and produces her biopic!

---

*as legend goes

QUEEN AMINA
1533-1610

*The Queen Whose Military
Prowess Expanded Zaria*

NATIONALITY	STAR SIGN	MOON SIGN
Nigerian	*Must have been a Leo*	*We're guessing Aries*

Epic Battle Cry

This queen was the definition of ruthless! Amina was a Hausa princess born in the mid-sixteenth century. Her family's immense wealth was built up through their trades business, keeping her living a lavish life of luxury. After her parents died and her brother took the throne, Amina said goodbye to traditions and threw herself into military warfare, gaining immense respect from the male-dominated military. When her brother died, Amina stepped up as the first ruling queen of her people. Her military prowess helped expand Zaria's territory to the mouth of Niger, which led to greater wealth for her and her people. Amina is also credited with the cultivation of kola nuts in the area that she ruled. The ferocious queen also invented the use of metal for warfare armour in Hausaland, as well as coming up with the idea to build mud walls and fortification around her territory, today known as Amina Walls. Rumour has it that Amina refused to marry and instead took a temporary husband after every battle before condemning him to death after they had sex . . . yikes!

WU ZETIAN
624AD-705AD

The Concubine Who Ruled An Entire Empire

NATIONALITY	STAR SIGN	MOON SIGN
Chinese	*Aquarius*	*Cancer*

"Remember, when one's aim is to achieve greatness . . . everyone is expendable."

As the only woman in more than 3,000 years of Chinese history to rule in her own right, Wu Zetian is nothing short of an enigma. From concubine to Empress, no one could foresee that the low-ranking teenager would have a chance to meet the Emperor, let alone become his equal. After a few short years (and suspicious deaths. . .), that is exactly what she did, remarkably sitting on a throne at equal elevation to that of her husband, Empress Gaozong. After his (suspicious) death, Wu Zetian ensured her sons would be placed in power, before ordering them to abdicate and taking the position herself. This ruthless ruler was surrounded by intense controversy in life as well as death, with one historian noting that "she is hated by gods and men alike". But can we expect anything less from a woman who defied all odds and snatched power at a time when her sex and rank deemed her unworthy? What we do know is that her reign was largely peaceful and prosperous, she was a strong advocate for meritocracy, she stabilised and consolidated the Tang dynasty, which is considered the golden age of Chinese civilisation. There were even rumours that she was one of the early promoters of printing! Good or bad, it's quite clear that Wu Zetian was one hell of a woman!

MEDIA
MOGULS

CRISSLE WEST

1982-

The Podcaster Breaking Generational
Trauma One "Read" At A Time

NATIONALITY	STAR SIGN	MOON SIGN
American	*Virgo*	*Virgo*

"Words mean things!"

Crissle West is the co-host of the hilarious podcast, The Read, along with the phenomenal Kidfury. Their podcast has undeniably helped to propel black-led podcasts into the mainstream arena, fetching millions of unique listeners every month. Throughout the course of the show, Crissle has been unapologetic, vulnerable and open, leading much-needed discussions on black and queer rights, as well as championing the need for therapy in the black community. Known for "reading" those who need to be checked and reminding us all that words do in fact "mean things", Crissle West uses her words to drive change in the world and in a society that so often tries to silence black women. We're so grateful that this one continues to give 'em hell!

ESTHER PEREL

1958-

The Woman Transforming The Way That We View Love

NATIONALITY	STAR SIGN	MOON SIGN
Belgian	*She must be a Cancer!*	*We're guessing Taurus. . .*

"We will have many relationships over the course of our lives. Some of us will have them with the same person."

Where should we begin? Dubbed the people's therapist, Esther Perel is a brilliant psychologist working to enlighten our approach to love and relationships. Perel was exposed early on in life to the complexities of the human psyche. Her parents were Nazi concentration camp survivors, and she noticed that amongst the survivors, there were "those who didn't die, and those who came back to life." Perel developed a concept called "erotic intelligence", the art of trusting yourself, being in touch with your own body, your boundaries, your values, and how you feel your own energy. She has helped thousands of relationships regain intimacy, healing and rebuild trust through her bestselling books, award-winning podcast and public talks. If there's a couch we wouldn't mind lounging on, it's hers!

HARRIET BEECHER STOWE
1811-1896

*The Little Woman Who Wrote The Book That
Started a Great War (thanks, Abraham Lincoln)*

NATIONALITY	STAR SIGN	MOON SIGN
American	*Gemini*	*Sagittarius*

"Women are the real architects of society."

We all know "Uncle Tom's Cabin"—if not because we've read it, it's certainly because of the splendid Siamese rendition displayed during Rodgers and Hammerstein's "The King and I". Harriet achieved national fame as she combined her passion for writing and literature with her interest and belief in the abolition of slavery. She expressed this world-changing view by writing "Uncle Tom's Cabin", a popular anti-slavery novel that highlighted sectionalism before the American Civil War. Being a social activist in her own right didn't ever stop her from doing what she loved in its entirety. Over her eighty-five years, Stowe wrote more than thirty books, both fiction and nonfiction, plus essays, poems, articles and hymns.

ISSA RAE

1985-

The Writer Bringing Black Narratives
to the Forefront

NATIONALITY	STAR SIGN	MOON SIGN
American	*Capricorn*	*Leo*

"I'm rooting for everybody black!"

Issa Rae, the patron saint of awkward black girls around the world, has worked to change the narrative for black stories. Issa grew tired of seeing inauthentic, stereotypical black characters in mainstream entertainment and so set out to solve the issue herself. Issa didn't let initial rejections from major networks stop her. Instead, she bravely stepped out on her own, creating the award-winning YouTube series, "The Misadventures of Awkward Black Girl". In due time, Issa stormed her way to the HBO writing room, delivering the instant-hit show "Insecure". Unapologetic about her love for the black community, Issa continues to support black projects and creatives, and this is why we'll always be rooting for her! Lovingly known for rapping in front of a mirror.

JUNE SARPONG OBE

1977-

The Woman Smashing Down Glass Ceilings

NATIONALITY	STAR SIGN	MOON SIGN
British	*Gemini*	*Scorpio*

> *"When you have equal opportunity coupled
> with self-belief, anything is possible."*

June Sarpong's illustrious career in broadcast media is just one of the many accolades held by the powerhouse. June is undeniably one of the most recognisable and dynamic faces of British television, featuring heavily in shows such as "The Pledge" and "Loose Women". Throughout the years, June has championed for increased diversity and inclusion in the media. Now the Director of Creative Diversity in the BBC, June hasn't shied away from being loud about her plans to revolutionise the creative space. Her fierce and empowering novel "Diversify", which highlights the consequences of continually marginalising groups within our society, has already begun to make waves, and we can't wait to see what's next. As Elton John once said, "You can tell everybody 'You're June Sarpong'". Get it? Not to worry. In-jokes with Elton himself are just another thing that only June can boast about!

LETITIA WRIGHT

1993-

The Actress Spreading Positivity
Everywhere She Goes

NATIONALITY	STAR SIGN	MOON SIGN
British	*Scorpio*	*Taurus*

"I'm not trying to be famous; I'm not trying to be the
next whatever. I'm just trying to be someone that
contributes positivity with my talent."

Letitia Wright is the incredibly talented actress who brought Shuri to life, introducing the world to Black Panther's stand-out character. In doing so, she highlighted the importance of black, female scientists across the world, whilst giving us the epic line, "Look at those!" Most actresses who hit it big with a blockbuster movie early on in their careers are eager for more, but not Letitia; she's ready to dive into "more wacky, deep arthouse films that make people think". Not only is the polished actress determined to contribute amazing content to the world, but she has also been open about her struggles with mental health. Letitia has openly discussed her battle with depression and credited her Christian faith for helping her out of dark times, making her an inspiration to many and a true superhero for all!

MARSAI MARTIN

2004-

*The Young Hollywood Executive
Producer Making History*

NATIONALITY	STAR SIGN	MOON SIGN
American	*Leo*	*Leo*

*"When I couldn't find characters for girls that
looked like me, I said: 'I will create them.'"*

Marsai Martin stole our hearts when she played the smart, cuttingly funny and, at times, devious Diane Johnson on ABC's hit comedy "Black-ish". The young star was not content with simply killing it in front of the camera; she was determined to shake it up behind the camera, too. Marsai went looking for support at ten years old when she pitched Little, a hilarious fantasy comedy, to her agents at the time, who sadly dismissed it as child's play. Ultimately, she got the last laugh when she fired them and made her dream come true— her way. This move landed her the impressive title of the youngest Hollywood executive producer in history. The film went on to rake in well over double its $20m budget! Adding further fuel to the fire, when asked where he saw Marsai in ten years, Kenya Barris, the creator of "Black-ish", responded with "my boss!"

OLIVIA WILDE

1984-

The Woman Pioneering Both In Front Of
And Behind The Camera Lens

NATIONALITY
American, British
and Irish

STAR SIGN
Pisces

MOON SIGN
Gemini

"Anything that becomes an obstacle in life
is only an opportunity to learn."

Most people recognise Olivia Wilde as an actress, most known for her role in "House", "The Girl Next Door" and even a short stint on our beloved "The O.C.", but what you may not know is that Olivia emerged as a fully formed filmmaker at the 2019 SXSW Film Festival with the world premiere of "Booksmart", in which her previously unnoticed directorial skills flourished. She has demonstrated both her production and acting skills in movies such as "Drinking Buddies" and "Meadowland". She has also explored her directing skills in the form of music as she directs music videos for artists such as Daft Punk and Red Hot Chili Peppers. We'd say that Olivia's directing career is definitely one to watch in the next few years. And she's made it very clear that acting is still very much something she will continue to pursue alongside this. A queen of killing multiple things at once—there isn't a clearer sign that we can kill it in more than one passion, too!

RADHIKA JONES

1973-

*The Editor Infusing Culture Into America's
Most Prestigious Publication*

NATIONALITY	STAR SIGN	MOON SIGN
Indian American	*Aquarius*	*Libra*

"My goal is to reflect the culture as I see it."

It's hard to believe that the phenomenal Radhika Jones was previously described as a long shot for the widely coveted Editor-in-Chief position at Vanity Fair. When the New York Times ran a piece speculating on who was going to take the post from the legendary Gloria Carter, of the eight hopefuls, Radhika Jones, the editorial director of the books department at the time, was not amongst them. Despite this, Jones rocketed through to the top position, tipping her hat at the confused expressions that followed. It's safe to say that the worldly Harvard graduate is poised to shake things up at the acclaimed publication, determined to bring a freshness to the magazine and ensure that it reflects the varied culture in the world. Since her appointment, Jones has already changed the game, featuring writer Lena Waithe in a simple white t-shirt with minimal to no makeup, rapper Kendrick Lamar in a hoodie, and heartthrob Idris Elba in a t-shirt, a marked change from the usual old-Hollywood glam. It was a move that brought a younger, more engaged and diverse audience to the magazine. One thing is certain, this self-professed re-reader is poised to deliver freshness to the publishing world!

VAMP

CHRISTINA OKOROCHA
RUBY ARYIKU
RUMBI MUPINDU

1994-   1993-   1993-

*The Three Women Looking To Solve The
Influencer Market's Diversity Problem*

NATIONALITY	STAR SIGN	MOON SIGN
British	*Capricorn*	*Aries*
British	*Libra*	*Capricorn*
British	*Libra*	*Capricorn*

*"It's not about us; it's about the work we do and the change
our work implements . . . we're more than happy to remain in
the background as long as the work is getting done."*

Diversity (or the lack thereof) in the influencer market is an issue that has come under the microscope recently—and for good reason! With brands set to spend $15bn by 2022 on influencer marketing, the vast majority of this growing pie goes exclusively to white influencers, despite the proven mutual benefit of increasing diversity in this space. Christina Okorocha, Ruby Aryiku and Rumbi Mupindu are looking to solve this issue via VAMP, a refreshing social media agency dedicated to representing the under-represented. Since its conception, VAMP has worked with a truly impressive clientele, such as Disney, Warner Brothers, Universal Pictures, Sony Music, Miss Guided, Benefit Cosmetics, Channel 4, HBO . . . need we go on? These girls are breaking down barriers across industries with new, innovative and culturally astute ways to bridge the gap between brands and diverse talent.

VICTORIA ALONSO

1965-

The Producer Who Brought Superheroes
To Life On The Big Screen

NATIONALITY	STAR SIGN	MOON SIGN
Argentine American	*Capricorn*	*Sagittarius*

> *"I think that women need to believe in their core that they're*
> *equal . . . you gotta believe it in your heart. You do."*

Chances are you've heard of one of Victoria Alonso's films. Alongside Kevin
Feige and Louis D'Esposito, Victoria is part of the holy trinity that runs
the billion-dollar franchise known as Marvel Studios. The Argentine-born
executive producer has worked on Marvel Studio Films since its inception
with Iron Man. As head of physical production, she is responsible for the
mind-blowing visual effects that have made Marvel films a must-see in cin-
ematic history. As one of the few Latinx women in the business, Victoria
champions for more inclusivity in the franchise. She fought for movies such
as "Black Panther" and is now gunning for the first openly gay superhero. In
her own words, the best thing about working in the Marvel universe is "to
be able to show new generations the characters that represent them in each
and every way." Victoria's amazing career is one for the books, but here's a
plot twist for you: the amazing executive didn't grow up watching Marvel. In
fact, she dabbled a little in their nemesis. "It was more DC Comics for me!"

POWERHOUSES

ENIOLA ALUKO

1987-

The Wayne Rooney of Women's Football

NATIONALITY	STAR SIGN	MOON SIGN
British Nigerian	*Taurus*	*Aquarius*

"I used to want to fit in,
now I don't mind standing out."

When someone says the name Eniola Aluko to anyone interested in women's football, there will often be many associations with "firsts", so Eniola can be described simply as a trailblazer. Eniola was the first female pundit on "Match of the Day" and the first female editor of "Woman's Hour", which enabled her to join the ranks of JK Rowling and Angelina Jolie. More importantly, she was also one of the first and most determined to expose the culture of discrimination within both football and the Football Association. While she was playing for the England women's team, the manager of the team warned Eniola to make sure her family did not bring the Ebola virus to Wembley. The undeniable trace of racism that would encourage someone to say such a sentence led Eniola to complain. There were two inquires, both of which concluded that the manager had done no wrong. Later on, the Department of Culture, Media and Sport convened a select committee and ruled the remarks as discriminatory. A move that will undoubtedly play a role in reshaping the long-standing industry in years to come. The sensational striker has since hung up her boots, a shame to those who will miss her roaring goals, but she says we should watch this space and she doesn't need to tell us twice!

MARY KOM

1983

The Legendary Boxer Knocking Down
Stereotypes One Medal At A Time

NATIONALITY	STAR SIGN	MOON SIGN
Indian	*Pisces*	*Libra*

"Never buy gold, simply earn it."

Mary Kom is a whirlwind boxer setting new standards in the world of boxing. Kom has defied societal expectations and excelled in a sport that was deemed unsuitable for a young Indian girl. Her all-in, aggressive style and impeccable timing have kept her ahead of the game with record-breaking accolades. The mother of three made an epic comeback after a short hiatus, and she is the first to admit that balancing her career with motherhood was nothing short of a struggle. Still, she remains determined to fight for everything she holds dear. The five-time World Amateur Boxing Champion is truly redefining the amateur boxing realm, fetching higher endorsements and awards than professional athletes without ever competing in professional boxing. As the only person, male or female, to win a medal in eight World Championships, we can say with true certainty that the champ is indeed here!

PRINCESS NOOR-UN-NISA INAYAT KHAN

1914-1944

The Princess Spy Who Helped Win The War

NATIONALITY	STAR SIGN	MOON SIGN
Indian	*Capricorn*	*Pisces*

"Liberté"

Princess Noor-un-nisa Inayat Khan lived an extraordinary life, as one would expect from the great-great-great granddaughter of Tipu Sultan, the Muslim ruler of the Kingdom of Mysore. She grew up travelling the globe, playing the harp and writing poetry. When World War II began, Noor and her family went to Britain to help with the war efforts. Her ability to speak French landed her a role as a radio operator in the Special Operation Executive. Although she received initial pushback due to her youth, inexperience and perceived carelessness, her excellent radio skills made her a necessity for the special forces. When all her fellow agents had been arrested, the princess refused to abandon ship. Instead, she proceeded to do the job of six radio operators on her own. At one time, her transmissions became the only link between agents in Paris and London, and her work has been described as crucial in aiding the escape of airmen and important deliveries. Noor was able to evade capture for three months, but eventually the Germans imprisoned, tortured and shot the princess. Her last words emphasised her motivations and beliefs, it was simply: "Liberté" . . . erm, does anyone have a tissue?

REBELS WITH
A CAUSE

CLAUDETTE COLVIN

1939-

The Girl Who Brought The
Revolution To Montgomery

NATIONALITY	STAR SIGN	MOON SIGN
American	*Virgo*	*Taurus*

"When it comes to justice, there is no easy way to get it.
You can't sugar-coat it. You have to take a stand and say, '
This is not right.' And I did."

Claudette Colvin was only fifteen years old when she refused to give up her seat on a crowded Alabama bus, nine months before Rosa Parks was forcibly hauled off a bus for doing the same thing. Colvin went on to challenge the law in court as one of four plaintiffs in the monumental Browder v. Gayle case, which successfully overturned bus segregation laws in Alabama. Whilst her actions were remarkable, the civil rights organisers questioned her appeal to the masses given her young age, darker skin tone and premarital pregnancy and so chose to uplift those with the "right" look. Eventually, her story was lost in history, but it's safe to say that her impact was limitless. A true rebel with one hell of a cause.

ISATOU CEESAY

1972-

The Environmentalist Empowering
Women With Plastic Recycling

NATIONALITY	STAR SIGN	MOON SIGN
Gambian	*Capricorn*	*Scorpio*

"When you abuse your environment, you abuse yourself."

Isatou Ceesay has certainly earned her title as the "Queen of Recycling". The Gambian activist is on a mission to educate women about the importance and benefits of recycling. Isatou dropped out of school at a young age, but her entrepreneurial spirit led her to solve one of the world's biggest problems. She founded the Recycling Centre of N'Jau to help educate her fellow Gambians about the environment. But she didn't stop there. She soon initiated a recycling movement called "One Plastic Bag" in the Gambia, which uniquely empowers women whilst protecting the environment. Every week, women craft wallets, bags and balls for children from the reclaimed plastic bags that surround the area. They are able to turn this waste plastic into revenue, thereby giving the women involved financial independence. She is a true queen of the people and the land!

MARLEY DIAS
2005-

The Girl Who Is Reshaping The Literary World

NATIONALITY	STAR SIGN	MOON SIGN
American	*Capricorn*	*Libra*

"I'm working to create a space where it feels easy to include and imagine black girls and make black girls like me the main characters of our lives."

Marley Dias is not only one of the cutest beings on the planet, but she's also one of the bravest. The young activist is taking on the centuries-old literary world and calling for an increase in children's books centred on more than the industry standard "white boy and his dog". She launched the #1000BlackGirlBooks campaign in 2015 with the goal of collecting and donating at least 1,000 books with black girl lead characters. The voracious reader has since surpassed this goal with thousands of diverse books circulating around the globe, including her very own book called "Marley Dias Gets it Done: And so can you!" With her signature colourful glasses and her heart-warming smile, Marley is for sure an inspiration to us all!

MIRIAM MAKEBA
1932-2008

The Woman Who Sang A Country To Freedom

NATIONALITY	STAR SIGN	MOON SIGN
South African	*Pisces*	*Scorpio*

"Age is wisdom, if one has lived one's life properly."

Miriam Makeba, affectionately known as "Mama Africa", was noted as the mother of the struggle by none other than Nelson Mandela himself. The South African songstress used her haunting melodies to not only voice the pain of a nation struggling under the hardship of an apartheid, but to also deliver hope to the nation's activists, many of who refer to her music as the soundtrack of their fight. The first black, African woman to win a Grammy, Makeba's incredible talent helped to broadcast South Africa's problems to the international world, an act that resulted in a thirty-year exile from her home country. There's no doubt that her life was large and colourful, with her five marriages coming in just shy of Elizabeth Taylors' seven, but slap on an impressive proposal from the president of Guinea (which she ended up turning down) and, dare we say, we may have levelled those scales!

SAMPAT PAL DEVI

1960-

The Vigilante In A Pink Saree Who Brought
Sticks To The Fight For Women's Rights

NATIONALITY	STAR SIGN	MOON SIGN
Indian	*Capricorn*	*Gemini*

"Village society in India is loaded against women. It refuses
to educate them, marries them off too early, barters them for
money. Village women need to study and become independent
to sort it out themselves."

Sampat Pal Devi has always been a fighter at heart, often getting in trouble as a young child for her naturally ferocious ways. The shepherd's daughter took life by the reins and taught herself to read when she was twelve. One day, she witnessed a neighbour beating his wife and asked him to stop. He refused. The next day, Sampat showed up with a group of women draped in pink sarees and armed with lathis (large bamboo sticks). They beat the man senseless. just as he had beat his wife, inadvertently starting the vigilante group known today as Gulabi Gang or the Pink Gang. The Gulabi Gang is dedicated to fighting (figuratively and literally) for women in India, protecting them, where the law so often fails, from violence and abuse. The gang has grown to over 400,000 members, with both men and women helping to support their cause. As with any gang, controversy is never too far away. Due to heavy criticism over the use of violence and charges of corruption, Sampat was eventually forced to step down as the leader of the group in 2014. She has since turned to politics, but her legacy continues to live on through the no-nonsense Gulabi Gang.

SYLVIA RIVERA

1951-2002

MARSH P. JOHNSON

1945-1992

The Women Who Helped Spur On The Gay Rights Movement

NATIONALITY	STAR SIGN	MOON SIGN
American	*Cancer*	*Gemini*
American	*Virgo*	*Pisces*

"Hell hath no fury like a drag queen scorned."

Sylvia and Marsha played vital roles in the iconic Stonewall riots that helped to launch the gay rights movement. Marsh P. Johnson (the P stands for "pay it no mind") was a colourful personality known for her blinding plastic heels and for sporting fruit, flowers and at times Christmas lights in her hair. The bold trans woman was said to be open and caring, with friends nicknaming her "Saint Marsha". In fact, Sylvia Rivera regarded her as the woman who saved her life. They didn't stop there. Following the events at Stonewall, they organised and participated in gay rights protests, as well as campaigning for AIDs awareness, the disease that devastated their community in the 1980s. The radiant activists even started Street Transvestite Action Revolutionaries, or STAR, a shelter for homeless LGBT youth, the first of its kind. Sadly, as trans women, they were repeatedly blocked from taking the helms of a movement that they helped to start. Rivera noted in a speech that "If it wasn't for the drag queen, there would be no gay liberation movement. We're the front-liners", she was consequently booed off the stage, an experience that resulted in a suicide attempt. Luckily, this was interrupted by Saint Marsha herself. Despite the challenges, the women stayed true to their cause until their deathbeds, with Sylvia urging gay leaders to prioritise inclusivity in the last hours of her life.

TARANA BURKE

1973-

*The Activist Who Changed The Conversation
On Sexual Assault When She Said "Me Too"*

NATIONALITY	STAR SIGN	MOON SIGN
American	*Virgo*	*Scorpio*

"You have to use your privilege to serve other people."

With one phrase, Tarana Burke sparked one of the most important conversations in recent history: "Me Too". The remarkable activist has dedicated her life to empowering survivors of sexual assault by giving them a voice and the resources to help move past their trauma. While she started the MeToo movement on Myspace, her campaign was catapulted to the public eye when actress Alyssa Milano unknowingly stumbled across the phrase and encouraged others to use it via her Twitter account, resulting in millions of retweets. Tarana has not let the virality of the movement stand in the way of the goal that she has spent decades working on. The activist remains dedicated to helping survivors heal and end sexual violence. She may not wear a cape, but Tarana Burke is certainly a hero in our eyes.

STEM-ETTERS

ANNIE EASLEY

1933-

The Mathematician Who Helped Us Understand The Solar System . . . And Paved The Way For The Prius!

NATIONALITY	STAR SIGN	MOON SIGN
American	*Taurus*	*Aries*

"If I can't work with you, I will work around you."

Annie Easley was literally out of this world. This mathematician, computer scientist and rocket scientist was a true pioneer. She not only navigated the unknown arena of space but also a society that was racially hostile to black women. Despite this, Easley worked above and beyond to make her incredible mark on the world. The outstanding mathematician helped to work on the Centaur rocket, which was used on the first American space probe to land on the moon, as well as the rocket that landed on Saturn. Her work as a programmer involved energy conversion systems. According to NASA, she "developed and implemented code" that led to the development of the battery used in the first hybrid cars. You're welcome, Prius drivers.

DR ELISABETH KÜBLER-ROSS
1926-2004

The Doctor Who Taught Us How To Grieve

NATIONALITY
Swiss

STAR SIGN
Cancer

MOON SIGN
Gemini

*"It's only when we truly know that we have a limited time
on earth that we will begin to live each day to the fullest,
as if it was the only one we had."*

Dr Elisabeth Kübler-Ross was a revolutionary psychiatrist who pioneered the study of death, dying and grief. Elisabeth defied expectations early on in life, resisting her father's wishes for her to settle into a comfortable career as a secretary in his business. She went on to pursue her aspirations of being a doctor after volunteering in hospitals during World War II at the ripe old age of sixteen! Inspired by her work with terminally ill patients, Elisabeth later wrote the ground-breaking novel "On Death and Dying", where she first introduced the Kübler-Ross Model, known today as the five stages of grief. Her progressive ideas have changed the way that we, as a society, view death. A life-changing contribution, if we do say so ourselves!

DR JANE C. WRIGHT

1919-2013

*The Woman Who Served
Cancer A Major Blow*

NATIONALITY	STAR SIGN	MOON SIGN
American	*Scorpio*	*Libra*

"Chemotherapy is the Cinderella of cancer research."

Dr Jane C. Wright is one of the most distinguished physician-scientists in modern medicine. Her career was punctuated with "firsts" for both her gender and her race. The pioneering doctor worked with her father at the Cancer Research Foundation in Harlem and began to research potential chemotherapeutic agents. Jane and her father were one of the first groups to report the use of nitrogen-mustard agents as a treatment of cancer, whilst also being the first to test folic acid antagonists as cancer treatments. Her contribution has notably pushed the field of chemotherapy forward, saving countless lives and helping us to kick cancer's butt one cell at a time!

DR HADIYAH-NICOLE GREEN

1983-

The Woman Poised to Eradicate Cancer
with Ground-breaking Tech

NATIONALITY	STAR SIGN	MOON SIGN
American	*Aquarius*	*Aquarius*

"It looks like I'm special, but I'm not. I'm no different from anybody else. When opportunity found me, I was prepared."

Taking on the impossible is simply a light day's work for Hadiyah-Nicole Green. The exceptional physicist has developed a new method for treating cancer that is considerably less harsh than chemotherapy. After losing her aunt and uncle to cancer, Green sought out a new way to eradicate the harrowing disease. Green's application of lasers and nanoparticles is still one of the most innovative treatments for cancer in medicine as it is able to identify the cancerous cells from the healthy ones and therefore will only attack the cancerous cells. This innovative idea saw Hadiyah hailed as the trailblazer of the year, as well as garnering her over a million in funding for her life-changing cancer treatment technology. With laser-sharp focus, Hadiyah is shaping up to change the world as we know it!

JENNIFER DOUDNA

1964-

The Scientist Who Discovered
The Gene-Editing Tool

NATIONALITY	STAR SIGN	MOON SIGN
American	*Pisces*	*Taurus*

"No one can take away those moments in the lab when we saw
something in nature that had never been seen before."

Jennifer Doudna is the brilliant biochemist who made one of the biggest and most important scientific discoveries in the modern age: CRISPR. This molecular tool makes use of a strange quirk in the immune system of bacteria that can edit genes in other organisms from plants to humans. CRISPR could revolutionise everything! Its potential is wide and varied, ranging from eradicating malaria to treating HIV to easing environmental stress via disease-resistant crops and plastic alternatives. This technology has opened up many possibilities and has even started a heated debate on the prospect of "designer babies", a conundrum that could stand to be one of the world's biggest ethical questions. How did Jennifer discover something with such a monumental impact? Well, at the heart of it is her unwavering love for science. Still a nerd at heart, Jennifer has been known to show up late to cocktail parties because she's spent too long on Skype discussing experiments with postdocs (in her evening gown, no less)! One thing we can all be sure of is that there is much more to come from that brilliant mind.

LINDA AVEY
1960-

ANNE WOJCICKI
1973-

The Women Making Genetic Data Accessible

NATIONALITY	STAR SIGN	MOON SIGN
American	*Aquarius*	*Sagittarius*
American	*Cancer*	*Scorpio*

"If you want to change this world, this community that we all live in, then get up and do it. And just start something."

You can thank Linda Avey and Anne Wojcicki for the trailblazer that is 23andMe. Along with their fellow co-founder, Paul Cusenza, these women created a company set out on a mission to make genetic testing consumer-friendly. 23andMe is the first and only company to offer genetic testing directly to its customers, as opposed to researchers and doctors. It was a move that has inspired many people across the world to grow curious about their own genetic makeup and how it has or will impact their lives. With millions of customers across the world, these women have definitely contributed to the genetic revolution.

WORLD
BUILDERS

ANNA HERINGER

1977-

*The Sustainable Architect Who
Is Making Mud Cool Again*

NATIONALITY
German

STAR SIGN
Libra

MOON SIGN
Libra

*"Three billion people on this planet live in buildings
made of mud, and with good reason!"*

A trailblazing German architect known for beautiful and sustainable buildings, such as the METI Handmade School in Rudrapur, Bangladesh. Along with Martin Rauch, Heringer helped to develop a new form of sustainable and highly effective design called "clay storming", a method that allows students to brainstorm without the waste of paper and pens. Known to drop gems like "sustainability = beauty", she has always been ahead of the trend!

ELSIE OWUSU OBE RIBA FRSA
1953

The Architect Building A More Inclusive Future

NATIONALITY	STAR SIGN	MOON SIGN
Ghanian	*Sagittarius*	*Capricorn*

> *"Discrimination . . . goes through architecture like a stick of rock. It's absolutely disgraceful, and it starts at the top. . . The whole thing needs shaking up."*

Elsie is an architect on a mission to open up the historically aloof profession. She fights to ensure that people other than the stereotypical white, middle-aged men are able to exceed in architecture. In addition to her campaign for inclusion in the architectural community, Elsie has also been involved in stunning projects in her homeland of Ghana, where she holds an artist-in-residence scheme. Her company, Just Ghana, also funds a monthly meal for 400 children and teachers in her father's home village of Konkonuru in Ghana. We have a lot of things to thank Elsie for, not least being the impeccable Green Park station!

NORMA MERRICK SKLAREK
1926-2012

The Architect Who Broke Through Many Firsts

NATIONALITY	STAR SIGN	MOON SIGN
American	*Aries*	*Gemini*

"In architecture, I had absolutely no role model. I'm happy today to be a role model for others that follow."

There's no doubt that Norma Merrick Sklarek was a first-mover. Throughout her illustrious architectural career, Norma was forced to break through a number of barriers. The first black woman to be a licensed architect in New York and California was just one of her many firsts. Facing systematic oppression for both her gender and race, Norma learned early on how to navigate the complicated, unpredictable and cruel space that is institutional discrimination. Despite this, she went on to co-found a woman-owned firm, Siegel Sklarek Diamond, which, at that time, was the largest woman-owned architectural firm in the United States. Her best-known projects include the Pacific Design Centre and terminal one at the Los Angeles International Airport, so next time you fly into LA, you know who to thank!

ZAHA HADID

1950-2016

The Woman Who Left Her Mark
On The Architectural Landscape

NATIONALITY	STAR SIGN	MOON SIGN
British-Iraqi	*Scorpio*	*Cancer*

"You have to really believe—not only in yourself; you have to believe that the world is actually worth your sacrifices."

Dame Zaha Hadid was a force to be reckoned with. The brilliant architect conquered the unwavering male-dominated field and left her mark across the globe with her unique and exquisite style. Shockingly, the Hadid nearly lost her career in 1995, when her daring design for Cardiff Bay was blocked by what's been described as an "alliance of narrow-minded politicians, peevish commentators and assorted dullards holding the Lottery purse strings". Dame Zaha Hadid then went on to make an epic comeback, cementing herself as one of the greatest architects of all time, winning back-to-back awards every year in the sixteen years leading up to her death and fourteen awards in one year alone—a record-breaker! Funnily enough, she ended up using that same rejected design for China's widely celebrated Guangzhou Opera House, which incidentally is still idolised today. Labelled as the Queen of the Curve for her daring and interesting building designs, Zaha Hadid actually lived in a non-curvy, relatively conventional building. Finally, not only did Zaha conquer the world of architecture, but she also dabbled in fashion, designing incredibly successful shoes and even partnering up with Pharrell Williams to design sleek trainers for his Adidas collection!

HONORARY
MENTIONS

AVA DUVERNAY
1972-

The Woman Carving Out New Doors
For All Film Creators To Use

NATIONALITY	STAR SIGN	MOON SIGN
American	*Virgo*	*Aquarius*

"I'm not going to continue knocking that old door that
doesn't open for me. I'm going to create my own
door and walk through that."

Ava DuVernay is history in the making. The Californian-born filmmaker first picked up a camera at the age of 32, a world-altering decision that would see her become the first black female filmmaker to be nominated for a Golden Globe, as well as a Best Picture Academy Award for the stunning *Selma*. Ava has made it crystal clear that her mission is to reshape the film industry so that everyone gets a chance to create. In 2010, the pioneering film mogul founded ARRAY, a collective focused on films by people of colour and women that has helped to bring a number of noteworthy projects to fruition. Ava's artistic productions have also been known to hold up a mirror to the harsh reality of our society and history through their thought-provoking ideologies. Moreover, her deliberate focus on the beauty of black bodies and the effervescence of black life in a space that typically disregards these attributes has not gone amiss. This spectacular woman is looking to reshape an industry that has secured its position in most homes of today, a task that we are eternally grateful for!

BEYONCÉ

1981-

*The Woman Who Sang The
Soundtrack To Our Lives*

NATIONALITY	STAR SIGN	MOON SIGN
American	*Virgo*	*Scorpio*

*"Your self-worth is determined by you. You don't have to
depend on someone telling you who you are."*

Beyoncé Giselle Knowles Carter needs no introduction. After years of pushing through impossible barriers, Beyoncé has certainly secured her legendary
status. The pioneering artist has done far more than create great music. She
has been active in pushing much-needed conversations and projects that have
worked to better the world. She spearheaded conversations on mental health
in the black community when she openly discussed her battle with depression
post-Destiny's Child's split. She is responsible for the addition of an entirely
new word (Bootylicious: defined as "sexually attractive, sexy, shapely") to
the Oxford English Dictionary. Her self-titled album, "Beyoncé", revolutionised the way artists release their work to the world. Her vast philanthropic
efforts are discreet but undeniably impactful. Did we forget anything? Oh!
She brought a future mogul/world leader, Blue Ivy, into the world. If that's
not the work of a Queen, we don't know what is!

NAOMI CAMPBELL
1970-

The Model Who Redefined Beauty

NATIONALITY	STAR SIGN	MOON SIGN
British	*Gemini*	*Sagittarius*

"Am I bossy? Absolutely. I don't like to lose, and if I'm told 'no,' then I find another way to get my 'yes.' But I'm a loyal person."

One of the five original supermodels, Naomi was born in London and has been at the top of the modelling game since she was fifteen years old. She has graced the covers of over 500 magazines and has been featured in campaigns for Burberry, Prada, Versace, Chanel, Dolce & Gabbana, Marc Jacobs, Louis Vuitton, Yves Saint Laurent and Valentino. She was the first black model to do . . . a lot, and she has earned her dues as an actress. She is most known for letting us know "she has her career!", despite always being willing to bring up other young, black models. She is a role model to us all. Literally.

RIHANNA

1988-

*The Mogul Who Has Revolutionised
Three Industries*

NATIONALITY	STAR SIGN	MOON SIGN
Barbadian	*Aquarius*	*Libra*

*"Let go of the things that make you feel dead!
Life is worth living!"*

Rihanna. One of the few women in the world recognisable by just one name. In her incredible lifetime, Rihanna (née Robyn Rihanna Fenty) has completely revolutionised not one, not two, but THREE major industries. Entering the music scene at the ripe age of sixteen, the pop songstress quickly proved that she was here to stay. She became the youngest solo artist to score fourteen number-one singles on the billboards (in record time, too!), selling over 54 million albums and 210 million tracks worldwide, earning her the title of bestselling digital artist of all time. Rihanna then moved onto her next industry: beauty. Her debut cosmetic line broke the mould with its wide and diverse range of skin tones, a true first of its kind, which saw the brand rack up $100 million in sales within the first few weeks! Rihanna then stepped into the fashion world with the FENTY luxury fashion line backed by LVMH. Notably, this is the first time that the conglomerate has launched a brand from inception since 1987. It's quite clear that whatever the Barbadian star touches turns to gold, and we think that definitely makes up for the fact that the adorable mogul can't wink!

SERENA WILLIAMS
1981-

The Woman Who Changed The Game Forever

NATIONALITY	STAR SIGN	MOON SIGN
American	*Libra*	*Virgo*

Serena Williams was three years old when she picked up her first tennis racket, and she has been dominating the sport ever since. With new players modelling their techniques after Serena and her older sister, Venus, it's no wonder why many have labelled the dynamic duo as the sisters who revamped the world of tennis. The powerful sportswoman has taken the game to new levels as she astonishingly pushed the limits of her physical prowess, providing reason, if there ever needed to be any, for why many call her the greatest athlete of all time. At every turn, Serena has had to battle racism and sexism. She was penalised more harshly than men for showing the same levels of passion for the game and drug tested at significantly higher rates than her white, female counterparts. It's obscenely clear that the world has not made it easy for this champion. Despite the odds, she has still come out as the true winner, smashing records throughout her career with thirty-nine Grand Slam titles under her belt—the record for any active player—and twenty-three Grand Slams as a single player, ten of which were gained in consecutive decades. It was an unprecedented accomplishment. If there's one thing we can say about Serena Williams, it's that she's completely unmatched!

SHONDA RHIMES

1970-

The Titan Who Owned A Night Of Network Television

NATIONALITY	STAR SIGN	MOON SIGN
American	*Capricorn*	*Aries*

"I think a lot of people dream. And while they are busy dreaming, the really happy people, the really successful people, the really interesting, powerful, engaged people? Are busy doing."

Unstoppable. Titan. Mogul. Just a few words used to describe the powerful force that is Shonda Rhimes, and we can tell you now that none of those do the multi-award-winning showrunner any justice. Born the last of six children to a family in Chicago, Illinois, Shonda's affinity for writing showed up early in life and soon ballooned into something unprecedented. The highest-paid showrunner in Hollywood is responsible for giving us the iconic "Princess Diaries 2", the sensational medical drama "Greys Anatomy", the heart-breaking "Private Practice", the nail-biting "Scandal", the addictive "How To Get Away With Murder"—phew, losing your breath already? Shonda has built up an entire empire from a series of back-to-back hit shows that at one time occupied 70 hours of network television, airing in 256 territories in 67 languages for an audience of 30 million people, a remarkable feat achieved by not a single soul before her. Shonda's genius ensured that she not only told exceptional stories but that the characters so often side-lined in mainstream TV found a home on the centre stage. Shonda made the most powerful person in US politics a black woman, proudly showcased gay love on our screens and normalised women in leadership positions. There's no question that Shonda Rhimes has changed the world. And with a mouth-watering Netflix deal to boot, we can't help but wonder where she'll take us next!

A NOTE FROM
THE PUBLISHER

Onwe is a black women-led publishing house and lifestyle business with a vision to amplify diverse voices and express under-represented ideals across all creative industries via unique content, products and experiences.

Find out more about us at: www.onwe.co

Follow us @weareonwe

A NOTE FROM
THE PUBLISHER